******

PASSWORD

logbook

BELONGS TO:

IMPORTANT REMINDER

Lock this logbook away from your computer in a drawer or a safe.

* * * * * *

PASSWORD logbook

• CONTENTS •

• TABLE OF CONTENTS •

Password Keeper

A - B

WEBSITE	*Page #*

C - D

WEBSITE	*Page #*

• TABLE OF CONTENTS •

Password Keeper

E-F

WEBSITE	*Page #*

G-H

WEBSITE	*Page #*

• TABLE OF CONTENTS •

I - J

WEBSITE	Page #

K - L

WEBSITE	Page #

• TABLE OF CONTENTS •

M - N

WEBSITE	Page #

O - P - Q

WEBSITE	Page #

• TABLE OF CONTENTS •

R - S

WEBSITE	*Page #*

T - U

WEBSITE	*Page #*

V - W

WEBSITE	Page #

X - Y - Z

WEBSITE	Page #

IMPORTANT REMINDER

Lock this logbook away from your computer in a drawer or a safe.

Password Keeper

WEBSITE:

Username:

Email Used:

PASSWORD:

Notes

WEBSITE:

Username:

Email Used:

PASSWORD:

Notes

WEBSITE:

Username:

Email Used:

PASSWORD:

Notes

Password Keeper

WEBSITE:

Username:

Email Used:

PASSWORD:

Notes

....

WEBSITE:

Username:

Email Used:

PASSWORD:

Notes

....

WEBSITE:

Username:

Email Used:

PASSWORD:

Notes

Password Keeper

WEBSITE:

Username:

Email Used:

PASSWORD:

Notes

....

WEBSITE:

Username:

Email Used:

PASSWORD:

Notes

....

WEBSITE:

Username:

Email Used:

PASSWORD:

Notes

Password Keeper

WEBSITE:

Username:

Email Used:

PASSWORD:

Notes

....

WEBSITE:

Username:

Email Used:

PASSWORD:

Notes

....

WEBSITE:

Username:

Email Used:

PASSWORD:

Notes

Password Keeper

WEBSITE:

Username:

Email Used:

PASSWORD:

Notes

....

WEBSITE:

Username:

Email Used:

PASSWORD:

Notes

....

WEBSITE:

Username:

Email Used:

PASSWORD:

Notes

Password Keeper

WEBSITE:

Username:

Email Used:

PASSWORD:

Notes

....

WEBSITE:

Username:

Email Used:

PASSWORD:

Notes

....

WEBSITE:

Username:

Email Used:

PASSWORD:

Notes

Password Keeper

WEBSITE:

Username:

Email Used:

PASSWORD:

Notes

WEBSITE:

Username:

Email Used:

PASSWORD:

Notes

WEBSITE:

Username:

Email Used:

PASSWORD:

Notes

Password Keeper

WEBSITE:

Username:

Email Used:

PASSWORD:

Notes

....

WEBSITE:

Username:

Email Used:

PASSWORD:

Notes

....

WEBSITE:

Username:

Email Used:

PASSWORD:

Notes

Password Keeper

WEBSITE:

Username:

Email Used:

PASSWORD:

Notes

....

WEBSITE:

Username:

Email Used:

PASSWORD:

Notes

....

WEBSITE:

Username:

Email Used:

PASSWORD:

Notes

Password Keeper

WEBSITE:

Username:

Email Used:

PASSWORD:

Notes

WEBSITE:

Username:

Email Used:

PASSWORD:

Notes

WEBSITE:

Username:

Email Used:

PASSWORD:

Notes

Password Keeper

WEBSITE:

Username:

Email Used:

PASSWORD:

Notes

WEBSITE:

Username:

Email Used:

PASSWORD:

Notes

WEBSITE:

Username:

Email Used:

PASSWORD:

Notes

Password Keeper

WEBSITE:

Username:

Email Used:

PASSWORD:

Notes

....

WEBSITE:

Username:

Email Used:

PASSWORD:

Notes

....

WEBSITE:

Username:

Email Used:

PASSWORD:

Notes

Password Keeper

WEBSITE:

Username:

Email Used:

PASSWORD:

Notes

....

WEBSITE:

Username:

Email Used:

PASSWORD:

Notes

....

WEBSITE:

Username:

Email Used:

PASSWORD:

Notes

Password Keeper

WEBSITE:

Username:

Email Used:

PASSWORD:

Notes

WEBSITE:

Username:

Email Used:

PASSWORD:

Notes

WEBSITE:

Username:

Email Used:

PASSWORD:

Notes

Password Keeper

WEBSITE:

Username:

Email Used:

PASSWORD:

Notes

....

WEBSITE:

Username:

Email Used:

PASSWORD:

Notes

....

WEBSITE:

Username:

Email Used:

PASSWORD:

Notes

Password Keeper

WEBSITE:

Username:

Email Used:

PASSWORD:

Notes

....

WEBSITE:

Username:

Email Used:

PASSWORD:

Notes

....

WEBSITE:

Username:

Email Used:

PASSWORD:

Notes

Password Keeper

WEBSITE:

Username:

Email Used:

PASSWORD:

Notes

....

WEBSITE:

Username:

Email Used:

PASSWORD:

Notes

....

WEBSITE:

Username:

Email Used:

PASSWORD:

Notes

Password Keeper

WEBSITE:

Username:

Email Used:

PASSWORD:

Notes

WEBSITE:

Username:

Email Used:

PASSWORD:

Notes

WEBSITE:

Username:

Email Used:

PASSWORD:

Notes

Password Keeper

WEBSITE:

Username:

Email Used:

PASSWORD:

Notes

WEBSITE:

Username:

Email Used:

PASSWORD:

Notes

WEBSITE:

Username:

Email Used:

PASSWORD:

Notes

Password Keeper

WEBSITE:

Username:

Email Used:

PASSWORD:

Notes

• • • •

WEBSITE:

Username:

Email Used:

PASSWORD:

Notes

• • • •

WEBSITE:

Username:

Email Used:

PASSWORD:

Notes

Password Keeper

WEBSITE:

Username:

Email Used:

PASSWORD:

Notes

....

WEBSITE:

Username:

Email Used:

PASSWORD:

Notes

....

WEBSITE:

Username:

Email Used:

PASSWORD:

Notes

Password Keeper

WEBSITE:

Username:

Email Used:

PASSWORD:

Notes

....

WEBSITE:

Username:

Email Used:

PASSWORD:

Notes

....

WEBSITE:

Username:

Email Used:

PASSWORD:

Notes

Password Keeper

WEBSITE:

Username:

Email Used:

PASSWORD:

Notes

....

WEBSITE:

Username:

Email Used:

PASSWORD:

Notes

....

WEBSITE:

Username:

Email Used:

PASSWORD:

Notes

Password Keeper

WEBSITE:

Username:

Email Used:

PASSWORD:

Notes

····

WEBSITE:

Username:

Email Used:

PASSWORD:

Notes

····

WEBSITE:

Username:

Email Used:

PASSWORD:

Notes

Password Keeper

WEBSITE:

Username:

Email Used:

PASSWORD:

Notes

WEBSITE:

Username:

Email Used:

PASSWORD:

Notes

WEBSITE:

Username:

Email Used:

PASSWORD:

Notes

Password Keeper

WEBSITE:

Username:

Email Used:

PASSWORD:

Notes

....

WEBSITE:

Username:

Email Used:

PASSWORD:

Notes

....

WEBSITE:

Username:

Email Used:

PASSWORD:

Notes

Password Keeper

WEBSITE:

Username:

Email Used:

PASSWORD:

Notes

....

WEBSITE:

Username:

Email Used:

PASSWORD:

Notes

....

WEBSITE:

Username:

Email Used:

PASSWORD:

Notes

Password Keeper

WEBSITE:

Username:

Email Used:

PASSWORD:

Notes

WEBSITE:

Username:

Email Used:

PASSWORD:

Notes

WEBSITE:

Username:

Email Used:

PASSWORD:

Notes

Password Keeper

WEBSITE:

Username:

Email Used:

PASSWORD:

Notes

....

WEBSITE:

Username:

Email Used:

PASSWORD:

Notes

....

WEBSITE:

Username:

Email Used:

PASSWORD:

Notes

Password Keeper

WEBSITE:

Username:

Email Used:

PASSWORD:

Notes

....

WEBSITE:

Username:

Email Used:

PASSWORD:

Notes

....

WEBSITE:

Username:

Email Used:

PASSWORD:

Notes

Password Keeper

WEBSITE:

Username:

Email Used:

PASSWORD:

Notes

....

WEBSITE:

Username:

Email Used:

PASSWORD:

Notes

....

WEBSITE:

Username:

Email Used:

PASSWORD:

Notes

Password Keeper

WEBSITE:

Username:

Email Used:

PASSWORD:

Notes

••••

WEBSITE:

Username:

Email Used:

PASSWORD:

Notes

••••

WEBSITE:

Username:

Email Used:

PASSWORD:

Notes

Password Keeper

WEBSITE:

Username:

Email Used:

PASSWORD:

Notes

....

WEBSITE:

Username:

Email Used:

PASSWORD:

Notes

....

WEBSITE:

Username:

Email Used:

PASSWORD:

Notes

Password Keeper

WEBSITE:

Username:

Email Used:

PASSWORD:

Notes

....

WEBSITE:

Username:

Email Used:

PASSWORD:

Notes

....

WEBSITE:

Username:

Email Used:

PASSWORD:

Notes

Password Keeper

WEBSITE:

Username:

Email Used:

PASSWORD:

Notes

....

WEBSITE:

Username:

Email Used:

PASSWORD:

Notes

....

WEBSITE:

Username:

Email Used:

PASSWORD:

Notes

Password Keeper

WEBSITE:

Username:

Email Used:

PASSWORD:

Notes

....

WEBSITE:

Username:

Email Used:

PASSWORD:

Notes

....

WEBSITE:

Username:

Email Used:

PASSWORD:

Notes

Password Keeper

WEBSITE:

Username:

Email Used:

PASSWORD:

Notes

....

WEBSITE:

Username:

Email Used:

PASSWORD:

Notes

....

WEBSITE:

Username:

Email Used:

PASSWORD:

Notes

Password Keeper

WEBSITE:

Username:

Email Used:

PASSWORD:

Notes

....

WEBSITE:

Username:

Email Used:

PASSWORD:

Notes

....

WEBSITE:

Username:

Email Used:

PASSWORD:

Notes

Password Keeper

WEBSITE:

Username:

Email Used:

PASSWORD:

Notes

....

WEBSITE:

Username:

Email Used:

PASSWORD:

Notes

....

WEBSITE:

Username:

Email Used:

PASSWORD:

Notes

Password Keeper

WEBSITE:

Username:

Email Used:

PASSWORD:

Notes

WEBSITE:

Username:

Email Used:

PASSWORD:

Notes

WEBSITE:

Username:

Email Used:

PASSWORD:

Notes

Password Keeper

WEBSITE:

Username:

Email Used:

PASSWORD:

Notes

....

WEBSITE:

Username:

Email Used:

PASSWORD:

Notes

....

WEBSITE:

Username:

Email Used:

PASSWORD:

Notes

Password Keeper

WEBSITE:

Username:

Email Used:

PASSWORD:

Notes

WEBSITE:

Username:

Email Used:

PASSWORD:

Notes

WEBSITE:

Username:

Email Used:

PASSWORD:

Notes

Password Keeper

WEBSITE:

Username:

Email Used:

PASSWORD:

Notes

....

WEBSITE:

Username:

Email Used:

PASSWORD:

Notes

....

WEBSITE:

Username:

Email Used:

PASSWORD:

Notes

Password Keeper

WEBSITE:

Username:

Email Used:

PASSWORD:

Notes

....

WEBSITE:

Username:

Email Used:

PASSWORD:

Notes

....

WEBSITE:

Username:

Email Used:

PASSWORD:

Notes

Password Keeper

WEBSITE:

Username:

Email Used:

PASSWORD:

Notes

....

WEBSITE:

Username:

Email Used:

PASSWORD:

Notes

....

WEBSITE:

Username:

Email Used:

PASSWORD:

Notes

Password Keeper

WEBSITE:

Username:

Email Used:

PASSWORD:

Notes

....

WEBSITE:

Username:

Email Used:

PASSWORD:

Notes

....

WEBSITE:

Username:

Email Used:

PASSWORD:

Notes

Password Keeper

WEBSITE:

Username:

Email Used:

PASSWORD:

Notes

WEBSITE:

Username:

Email Used:

PASSWORD:

Notes

WEBSITE:

Username:

Email Used:

PASSWORD:

Notes

Password Keeper

WEBSITE:

Username:

Email Used:

PASSWORD:

Notes

....

WEBSITE:

Username:

Email Used:

PASSWORD:

Notes

....

WEBSITE:

Username:

Email Used:

PASSWORD:

Notes

Password Keeper

WEBSITE:

Username:

Email Used:

PASSWORD:

Notes

....

WEBSITE:

Username:

Email Used:

PASSWORD:

Notes

....

WEBSITE:

Username:

Email Used:

PASSWORD:

Notes

Password Keeper

WEBSITE:

Username:

Email Used:

PASSWORD:

Notes

....

WEBSITE:

Username:

Email Used:

PASSWORD:

Notes

....

WEBSITE:

Username:

Email Used:

PASSWORD:

Notes

Password Keeper

WEBSITE:

Username:

Email Used:

PASSWORD:

Notes

....

WEBSITE:

Username:

Email Used:

PASSWORD:

Notes

....

WEBSITE:

Username:

Email Used:

PASSWORD:

Notes

Password Keeper

WEBSITE:

Username:

Email Used:

PASSWORD:

Notes

....

WEBSITE:

Username:

Email Used:

PASSWORD:

Notes

....

WEBSITE:

Username:

Email Used:

PASSWORD:

Notes

Password Keeper

WEBSITE:

Username:

Email Used:

PASSWORD:

Notes

....

WEBSITE:

Username:

Email Used:

PASSWORD:

Notes

....

WEBSITE:

Username:

Email Used:

PASSWORD:

Notes

Password Keeper

WEBSITE:

Username:

Email Used:

PASSWORD:

Notes

....

WEBSITE:

Username:

Email Used:

PASSWORD:

Notes

....

WEBSITE:

Username:

Email Used:

PASSWORD:

Notes

Password Keeper

WEBSITE:

Username:

Email Used:

PASSWORD:

Notes

....

WEBSITE:

Username:

Email Used:

PASSWORD:

Notes

....

WEBSITE:

Username:

Email Used:

PASSWORD:

Notes

Password Keeper

WEBSITE:

Username:

Email Used:

PASSWORD:

Notes

....

WEBSITE:

Username:

Email Used:

PASSWORD:

Notes

....

WEBSITE:

Username:

Email Used:

PASSWORD:

Notes

Password Keeper

WEBSITE:

Username:

Email Used:

PASSWORD:

Notes

....

WEBSITE:

Username:

Email Used:

PASSWORD:

Notes

....

WEBSITE:

Username:

Email Used:

PASSWORD:

Notes

Password Keeper

WEBSITE:

Username:

Email Used:

PASSWORD:

Notes

....

WEBSITE:

Username:

Email Used:

PASSWORD:

Notes

....

WEBSITE:

Username:

Email Used:

PASSWORD:

Notes

Password Keeper

WEBSITE:

Username:

Email Used:

PASSWORD:

Notes

....

WEBSITE:

Username:

Email Used:

PASSWORD:

Notes

....

WEBSITE:

Username:

Email Used:

PASSWORD:

Notes

Password Keeper

WEBSITE:

Username:

Email Used:

PASSWORD:

Notes

....

WEBSITE:

Username:

Email Used:

PASSWORD:

Notes

....

WEBSITE:

Username:

Email Used:

PASSWORD:

Notes

Password Keeper

WEBSITE:

Username:

Email Used:

PASSWORD:

Notes

••••

WEBSITE:

Username:

Email Used:

PASSWORD:

Notes

••••

WEBSITE:

Username:

Email Used:

PASSWORD:

Notes

Password Keeper

WEBSITE:

Username:

Email Used:

PASSWORD:

Notes

....

WEBSITE:

Username:

Email Used:

PASSWORD:

Notes

....

WEBSITE:

Username:

Email Used:

PASSWORD:

Notes

Password Keeper

WEBSITE:

Username:

Email Used:

PASSWORD:

Notes

....

WEBSITE:

Username:

Email Used:

PASSWORD:

Notes

....

WEBSITE:

Username:

Email Used:

PASSWORD:

Notes

Password Keeper

WEBSITE:

Username:

Email Used:

PASSWORD:

Notes

....

WEBSITE:

Username:

Email Used:

PASSWORD:

Notes

....

WEBSITE:

Username:

Email Used:

PASSWORD:

Notes

Password Keeper

WEBSITE:

Username:

Email Used:

PASSWORD:

Notes

····

WEBSITE:

Username:

Email Used:

PASSWORD:

Notes

····

WEBSITE:

Username:

Email Used:

PASSWORD:

Notes

Password Keeper

WEBSITE:

Username:

Email Used:

PASSWORD:

Notes

WEBSITE:

Username:

Email Used:

PASSWORD:

Notes

WEBSITE:

Username:

Email Used:

PASSWORD:

Notes

Password Keeper

WEBSITE:

Username:

Email Used:

PASSWORD:

Notes

....

WEBSITE:

Username:

Email Used:

PASSWORD:

Notes

....

WEBSITE:

Username:

Email Used:

PASSWORD:

Notes

Password Keeper

WEBSITE:

Username:

Email Used:

PASSWORD:

Notes

....

WEBSITE:

Username:

Email Used:

PASSWORD:

Notes

....

WEBSITE:

Username:

Email Used:

PASSWORD:

Notes

Password Keeper

WEBSITE:

Username: ______

Email Used: ______

PASSWORD: ______

______

Notes

....

WEBSITE:

Username: ______

Email Used: ______

PASSWORD: ______

______

Notes

....

WEBSITE:

Username: ______

Email Used: ______

PASSWORD: ______

______

Notes

Password Keeper

WEBSITE:

Username:

Email Used:

PASSWORD:

Notes

....

WEBSITE:

Username:

Email Used:

PASSWORD:

Notes

....

WEBSITE:

Username:

Email Used:

PASSWORD:

Notes

Password Keeper

WEBSITE:

Username:

Email Used:

PASSWORD:

Notes

....

WEBSITE:

Username:

Email Used:

PASSWORD:

Notes

....

WEBSITE:

Username:

Email Used:

PASSWORD:

Notes

Password Keeper

WEBSITE:

Username:

Email Used:

PASSWORD:

Notes

....

WEBSITE:

Username:

Email Used:

PASSWORD:

Notes

....

WEBSITE:

Username:

Email Used:

PASSWORD:

Notes

Password Keeper

WEBSITE:

Username:

Email Used:

PASSWORD:

Notes

••••

WEBSITE:

Username:

Email Used:

PASSWORD:

Notes

••••

WEBSITE:

Username:

Email Used:

PASSWORD:

Notes

Password Keeper

WEBSITE:

Username:

Email Used:

PASSWORD:

Notes

....

WEBSITE:

Username:

Email Used:

PASSWORD:

Notes

....

WEBSITE:

Username:

Email Used:

PASSWORD:

Notes

Password Keeper

WEBSITE:

Username:

Email Used:

PASSWORD:

Notes

....

WEBSITE:

Username:

Email Used:

PASSWORD:

Notes

....

WEBSITE:

Username:

Email Used:

PASSWORD:

Notes

Password Keeper

WEBSITE:

Username:

Email Used:

PASSWORD:

Notes

WEBSITE:

Username:

Email Used:

PASSWORD:

Notes

WEBSITE:

Username:

Email Used:

PASSWORD:

Notes

Password Keeper

WEBSITE:

Username:

Email Used:

PASSWORD:

Notes

WEBSITE:

Username:

Email Used:

PASSWORD:

Notes

WEBSITE:

Username:

Email Used:

PASSWORD:

Notes

Password Keeper

WEBSITE:

Username:

Email Used:

PASSWORD:

Notes

....

WEBSITE:

Username:

Email Used:

PASSWORD:

Notes

....

WEBSITE:

Username:

Email Used:

PASSWORD:

Notes

Password Keeper

WEBSITE:

Username:

Email Used:

PASSWORD:

Notes

WEBSITE:

Username:

Email Used:

PASSWORD:

Notes

WEBSITE:

Username:

Email Used:

PASSWORD:

Notes

Password Keeper

WEBSITE:

Username:

Email Used:

PASSWORD:

Notes

WEBSITE:

Username:

Email Used:

PASSWORD:

Notes

WEBSITE:

Username:

Email Used:

PASSWORD:

Notes

Password Keeper

WEBSITE:

Username:

Email Used:

PASSWORD:

Notes

....

WEBSITE:

Username:

Email Used:

PASSWORD:

Notes

....

WEBSITE:

Username:

Email Used:

PASSWORD:

Notes

Password Keeper

WEBSITE:

Username:

Email Used:

PASSWORD:

Notes

....

WEBSITE:

Username:

Email Used:

PASSWORD:

Notes

....

WEBSITE:

Username:

Email Used:

PASSWORD:

Notes

Password Keeper

WEBSITE:

Username:

Email Used:

PASSWORD:

Notes

WEBSITE:

Username:

Email Used:

PASSWORD:

Notes

WEBSITE:

Username:

Email Used:

PASSWORD:

Notes

Password Keeper

WEBSITE:

Username:

Email Used:

PASSWORD:

Notes

....

WEBSITE:

Username:

Email Used:

PASSWORD:

Notes

....

WEBSITE:

Username:

Email Used:

PASSWORD:

Notes

Password Keeper

WEBSITE:

Username:

Email Used:

PASSWORD:

Notes

....

WEBSITE:

Username:

Email Used:

PASSWORD:

Notes

....

WEBSITE:

Username:

Email Used:

PASSWORD:

Notes

Password Keeper

WEBSITE:

Username:

Email Used:

PASSWORD:

Notes

WEBSITE:

Username:

Email Used:

PASSWORD:

Notes

WEBSITE:

Username:

Email Used:

PASSWORD:

Notes

WEBSITE:

Username:

Email Used:

PASSWORD:

Notes

....

WEBSITE:

Username:

Email Used:

PASSWORD:

Notes

....

WEBSITE:

Username:

Email Used:

PASSWORD:

Notes

Password Keeper

WEBSITE:

Username:

Email Used:

PASSWORD:

Notes

....

WEBSITE:

Username:

Email Used:

PASSWORD:

Notes

....

WEBSITE:

Username:

Email Used:

PASSWORD:

Notes

Password Keeper

WEBSITE:

Username:

Email Used:

PASSWORD:

Notes

....

WEBSITE:

Username:

Email Used:

PASSWORD:

Notes

....

WEBSITE:

Username:

Email Used:

PASSWORD:

Notes

Password Keeper

WEBSITE:

Username:

Email Used:

PASSWORD:

Notes

....

WEBSITE:

Username:

Email Used:

PASSWORD:

Notes

....

WEBSITE:

Username:

Email Used:

PASSWORD:

Notes

Password Keeper

WEBSITE:

Username:

Email Used:

PASSWORD:

Notes

....

WEBSITE:

Username:

Email Used:

PASSWORD:

Notes

....

WEBSITE:

Username:

Email Used:

PASSWORD:

Notes

Password Keeper

WEBSITE:

Username:

Email Used:

PASSWORD:

Notes

....

WEBSITE:

Username:

Email Used:

PASSWORD:

Notes

....

WEBSITE:

Username:

Email Used:

PASSWORD:

Notes

Password Keeper

WEBSITE:

Username:

Email Used:

PASSWORD:

Notes

....

WEBSITE:

Username:

Email Used:

PASSWORD:

Notes

....

WEBSITE:

Username:

Email Used:

PASSWORD:

Notes

Password Keeper

WEBSITE:

Username:

Email Used:

PASSWORD:

Notes

....

WEBSITE:

Username:

Email Used:

PASSWORD:

Notes

....

WEBSITE:

Username:

Email Used:

PASSWORD:

Notes

Password Keeper

WEBSITE:

Username:

Email Used:

PASSWORD:

Notes

....

WEBSITE:

Username:

Email Used:

PASSWORD:

Notes

....

WEBSITE:

Username:

Email Used:

PASSWORD:

Notes

Password Keeper

WEBSITE:

Username:

Email Used:

PASSWORD:

Notes

....

WEBSITE:

Username:

Email Used:

PASSWORD:

Notes

....

WEBSITE:

Username:

Email Used:

PASSWORD:

Notes

Password Keeper

WEBSITE:

Username:

Email Used:

PASSWORD:

Notes

....

WEBSITE:

Username:

Email Used:

PASSWORD:

Notes

....

WEBSITE:

Username:

Email Used:

PASSWORD:

Notes

Password Keeper

WEBSITE:

Username:

Email Used:

PASSWORD:

Notes

••••

WEBSITE:

Username:

Email Used:

PASSWORD:

Notes

••••

WEBSITE:

Username:

Email Used:

PASSWORD:

Notes

Password Keeper

WEBSITE:

Username:

Email Used:

PASSWORD:

Notes

....

WEBSITE:

Username:

Email Used:

PASSWORD:

Notes

....

WEBSITE:

Username:

Email Used:

PASSWORD:

Notes

Password Keeper

WEBSITE:

Username:

Email Used:

PASSWORD:

Notes

....

WEBSITE:

Username:

Email Used:

PASSWORD:

Notes

....

WEBSITE:

Username:

Email Used:

PASSWORD:

Notes

Made in the USA
Monee, IL
04 November 2026

67377420R00066